NATIONAL
GEOGRAPHIC
KiDS

ANIMAL JAM

ANIMAL HANDBOOK

YOUR GUIDE TO THE AWESOME ANIMALS AND FANTASTIC FASHIONS OF JAMAA

NATASHA LEVINGER

NATIONAL GEOGRAPHIC
WASHINGTON, D.C.

TABLE OF CONTENTS

WELCOME TO

THE ONLINE GAME FOR
KIDS WHO LOVE ANIMALS!

GET READY TO EXPLORE A WILD WORLD
WHERE YOU GET TO BECOME YOUR FAVORITE ANIMAL ...

In this live, multiplayer, online playground, you'll travel to the world of Jamaa to play games, meet new buddies, throw parties, explore awesome lands, and so much more—all while learning incredible info about animals. It's a world that's fun, educational, and THE place to be for kids who love animals and the outdoors.

There's so much to discover in Animal Jam, and that's where handbooks such as this one come in. It's filled with facts and tips that will help make your experience even wilder. Within these pages, you'll find out what kinds of animals live in Jamaa, uncover behind-the-scenes secrets, and learn how to take your gameplay to the next level. The answers are all here!

SO, JAMMERS: Grab your handbook, log in, and get ready to become the coolest creature in Animal Jam!

PLAY SAFE

ANIMAL JAM IS A SAFE ONLINE ENVIRONMENT. But whenever you use the Internet, there are rules you need to follow to keep yourself and others safe:

1 **Never** share your real name, age, phone number, or home and email addresses with anyone online. Only share information that your parents say is OK to share.

2 **Never ever** give anyone your password. Somebody might promise to give you something cool if you give them your password. Don't do it. It's a trick!

3 **Never** meet anyone in person who you met on the Internet. Sometimes people aren't honest about who they really are.

4 **Always** be kind to everyone. Be friendly to other players and help us keep Animal Jam a happy place.

PLAY WILD ON THE GO!

There's more than one way to visit Jamaa, which makes the fun almost endless! Animal Jam – Play Wild! is the supercool mobile version of the game that has tons of the fun of Animal Jam, plus a few unique surprises. Read on to discover awesome info about Play Wild.

WHO are the ANiMaLs OF JaMaa?

WHEN YOU SET PAW IN JAMAA, YOU'RE GOING TO MEET LOTS OF OTHER COOL CREATURES. You'll be exploring the savanna, trekking through the jungle, or even diving under the waves, so who knows what you might discover! But just who are these wild animals that smile, dance, and play all day?

JAMAA WAS ONCE FILLED WITH HUNDREDS OF ANIMAL SPECIES OF ALL SHAPES AND SIZES. Mira and Zios, the two guardian spirits of Jamaa, gifted every animal species a Heartstone, a jewel containing the essence of that species. For many years, all the animals of Jamaa worked together. But when some species grew distrustful of one another, the animals separated into isolated villages and took their Heartstones with them.

With Jamaa so divided, the dark Phantoms invaded, bringing pollution and destruction. Soon, they had destroyed most of Jamaa and had stolen away many species' Heartstones, causing those species to disappear from Jamaa! To save their precious land, Mira and Zios, along with the Alphas and the remaining animals in Jamaa, waged an epic battle. When it was over, the Phantoms had been driven from the land. Over time, some of the lost and stolen Heartstones were brought back to Jamaa, making it possible for those animal species to live there. Learning from past mistakes, the animals worked together to return their home to a place of peace and tranquility.

Now that you are a member of the Jamaa community, it is up to you to keep the Phantoms away as you restore and beautify Jamaa. As a Jammer, you can work against the Phantoms by going on Adventures and playing games, as well as by learning about the animals of Jamaa and animals in the wild. Throughout Jamaa's lands and oceans, there are tons of videos, photos, and fun facts about all sorts of animals. You'll learn not only amazing things about animals, but also how to keep them safe—helping you help animals everywhere!

EXPLORE THE LANDS AND OCEANS OF JAMAA

IN JAMAA, THERE ARE MANY EXCEPTIONAL ECOSYSTEMS TO DISCOVER (and more are found from time to time). Each land and ocean is based on a real environment in the wild. But to explore them all, you might need some special creatures:

sarepia Forest

ON LAND: There are nine lands: Jamaa Township, Appondale, Mt. Shiveer, the Lost Temple of Zios, Balloosh, Sarepia Forest, Coral Canyons, Crystal Sands, and Kimbara Outback. As long as you can walk (or hop!), you can visit any of these lands.

IN THE SKY: Several lands have cool shops or places to visit that are wings-only. And there's nothing like a bird's-eye view of Jamaa!

Royal Ridge

UNDER THE WAVES: There are four oceans: Bahari Bay, Crystal Bay, Kani Cove, and Deep Blue. Only swimming animals can visit the oceans, but that doesn't mean it's off-limits to animals with legs. Some animals, such as polar bears, penguins, and otters, are comfortable in and out of the water.

Kani Cove

BecomE AN aNiMaL!

JAMAA IS BURSTING WITH SO MANY COOL CREATURES THAT IT MIGHT FEEL IMPOSSIBLE TO CHOOSE JUST ONE. The best part is ... you don't have to! Members can choose to be as many as 1,000 animals, all with different personalities, styles, and looks. Feel like being a bunny one day and an eagle the next? You can show all sides of yourself in Jamaa!

J AMMERS BECOME THEIR VERY FIRST ANIMAL WHEN FIRST LOGGING IN TO ANIMAL JAM. To help you find the perfect moniker, a name generator will help you select three parts to your name. Use the **arrow buttons** above and below the names to switch up the words, or click the **randomizer lever** on the side.

CHoose aN ANiMaL

Monkey

create a NaMe

Countess	Green	fruit
Cranky	Grumpy	gem
Crashing	**Happy**	**ghost**
Creature	Hiking	giraffe
Crouching	Icy	girl

ARROW BUTTONS

RANDOMIZER LEVER

Crashing Happyghost

YOUR NAME

NOT QUITE SURE WHICH CREATURE SHARES YOUR FEATURES? CHECK OUT THESE TERRIFIC TIPS:

1. GO WITH YOUR FAVORITE WILD ANIMAL.

Choose one that matches your personality. Are you a fearless adventurer? Maybe a monkey is the best fit for you. Do you make decisions slowly and carefully? A sloth might be just your speed.

2. PICK AN ANIMAL THAT MATCHES YOUR CURRENT MOOD.

Are you filled with energy and bouncing off the walls? Sounds like you could be a bunny!

3. SELECT AN ANIMAL THAT MEANS SOMETHING TO YOU.

Does your beloved kitty never leave your side? Perhaps pick a wild cat, such as a tiger or lion.

THIS iS WHERE YOU'LL SEE IF AN ANIMAL IS UNAVAILABLE.

ANiMaL AVAiLaBiLiTY

Some animals might have a banner over their picture that says **"traveling."** That means you can't become these animals right now. Don't worry, though: These migratory creatures always come home eventually! When animals return to Jamaa, they have a banner that says **"new"** on their picture. There are also animals that are **"endangered."** Just like in the wild, sometimes animals in Jamaa can become endangered. If animals have an "endangered" banner, you can't become one right now. But they may return to Jamaa at some point, so keep your eyes open.

CHANGE YOUR LOOK

SHOWING OFF YOUR SIGNATURE STYLE IS ONE OF THE BEST PARTS OF ANIMAL JAM. Are you heading out to a party, having a chill night in your den, or planning to spend the day at the beach? Your animal can reflect whatever part of your personality you feel like expressing that day—or even that hour!

O START CUSTOMIZING, CLICK YOUR **ANIMAL PICTURE** IN THE LOWER LEFT-HAND CORNER OF YOUR SCREEN. There are tons of options to choose from and trillions of possible customization combinations!

COLOR OPTIONS

PATTERN OPTIONS

EYE OPTIONS

COLOR

Some animals come with default colors that aren't available once you swap them out with another color. For instance, arctic wolves have a default undercoat that is light gray; once you change this color, it can't be chosen again. The same is true for other animals like sheep, polar bears, and goats. Before switching colors, make sure you don't want to keep the one the animal comes with!

eyes

You can pick cool eye shapes and colors that are as unique as you are. Ever wanted purple eyes with long eyelashes? Now's your chance!

INSIDER INFO

SOMETIMES ANIMALS WITH SPECIAL PATTERNS appear in Jamaa for a limited time. For example, snowflake arctic wolves once came to Jamaa. These special arctic wolves had a beautiful snowflake pattern on their fur, and a trail of snowflakes followed them wherever they walked!

Patterns

Every animal in Jamaa is special. As you explore, you might notice some animals sporting different patterns and colors. Blotches, spots, leaves, crescent moons, and stars are patterns that can be found only on land animals. Hibiscus, short stripes, skulls, flowers, and sea stars are patterns that can be found only on ocean animals. And remember, more animals with amazing features are arriving in Jamaa all the time!

Change your Look in Play Wild!

You're playing Animal Jam on your mobile device and you just bought an amazing rare item from the Sapphire Shop! Awesome! So how do you change your look? Just tap your **animal icon** in the lower left-hand corner of your screen and you'll head to the customization screen. From here you can choose from tons of cool colors, go shopping for new accessories, and even save different outfits for easy access later. You can swipe on your animal to rotate it and see how your new style looks from every angle, and you can tap the **magnifying glass** in the upper right-hand corner to zoom in.

JAMAA'S AMAZING ANIMALS

Get ready to discover everything about the animals you can become, their signature moves, the secret places they can visit, and more. You'll also learn all about their counterparts in the wild, some of their special qualities, and how you can help keep them safe. Will you soar through the sky? Frolic through the forest? Dive into the depths? Turn the page to get started!

Meet the LAND ANIMALS

In the wild, land animals make up only 0.4 percent of the entire animal kingdom! But here in Jamaa, these critters are king. Check out the map to see where your favorites crawl, climb, and swing across the screen!

EXPLORE THE LANDS OF JAMAA

BALLOOSH

CORAL CANYONS

Mt. SHiveer

SAREPIA FOREST

JAMAA TOWNSHIP

APPONDALE

CRYSTAL SANDS

LOST TEMPLE OF ZIOS

KIMBARA OUTBACK

JAMAA TOWNSHIP *(City)*

Jamaa Township is the hub of Jamaa's action and where new Jammers enter to begin their adventures. Like residents of cities and village centers all over the world, Jammers gather here to shop, play, and hang out. In the wild, urban centers like Jamaa Township are home to many animals that have adapted to life there. Some you may be familiar with are pigeons, raccoons, and even coyotes that live near you.

CRYSTAL SANDS *(Seashore)*

Whether the shore is sandy or rocky, many wild animals live in this unique habitat at the water's edge. Seals sun themselves on the sand, and sea turtles nest on the shore. And others, such as hermit crabs, toddle through tide pools. The beaches of Crystal Sands are great for sunbathing, but are even better for learning about marine life at Tierney's Aquarium.

CORAL CANYONS *(Desert)*

Even though one-third of the world is desert, not all are the endless dunes of sand you might envision. There are cold deserts and hot deserts, high deserts and low deserts. Depending on the kind of desert, the types of life found there can be very different— from arctic foxes and lichen in the Arctic tundra to cacti and scorpions in hot deserts. In Coral Canyons you'll find some of these plants and animals, as well as an epic waterfall and the Art Studio where you can capture the desert beauty!

EXPLORE THE LANDS OF JAMAA

MT. SHIVEER *(Mountain)*
High mountain terrains are extreme places, and the animals that live there need to be tough enough to withstand limited food availability, extreme weather, and precarious footing. In Mt. Shiveer you'll find a frozen ice patch and ice slides, as well as the Hot Cocoa Hut, where you can warm up!

APPONDALE *(Savanna)*
The savanna of Appondale most resembles the vast grasslands found in Africa. On them you can find wild wildebeest grazing on the grass, and too-hot elephants, warthogs, and rhinos wading into mud pools to cool off. Be sure to climb the giant tree in Appondale where you'll have a bird's-eye view of all the savanna animals wandering by.

SAREPIA FOREST *(Temperate Forest)*
Tall trees loom high above the forest floor, part of a complex forest ecosystem that also includes animals like deer and foxes, as well as plants, soil, and microscopic organisms. Journey to Sarepia Forest to experience arboreal life in the treetops—or come back down to ground level to sit around the campfire.

INSIDER INFO
THE ADVENTURE BASE CAMP IS JUST FOR LAND AND FLYING ANIMALS. You can access it through a tunnel in the Lost Temple of Zios or from your Party List. Some Adventures are available to all animals, whereas others are just for members, flying animals, or specific species.

LOST TEMPLE OF ZIOS *(Rain Forest)*

Tropical rain forests are teeming with flora and fauna. In fact, half of all the species on the planet live there! In the wild, this lush environment is home to curious and colorful animals and plants, including bright blue poison dart frogs and orchids of every shade. In the Lost Temple of Zios you can see tropical fauna and flora and then learn more about animals of all kinds in the Chamber of Knowledge.

KIMBARA OUTBACK *(Outback)*

Kimbara Outback resembles the interior wilderness of Australia. This area—called the outback—is about 2.5 million square miles (6.5 million sq km) with a climate that is mostly warm and dry. All kinds of fascinating animals call the Australian outback home, including dingoes, kangaroos, wallabies, wild camels, snakes, lizards, and about 2,000 species of spiders!

BALLOOSH *(Wetland)*

Whether it's called a swamp, marsh, bog, pond, or river delta, these excellent ecosystems all have one thing in common: they're all wetlands! These low-lying lands covered by fresh or salt water may take many forms, but all wild wetlands are super-important habitats to the animals and people that call them home. They can even house a treasure trove of Earth's history. In Jamaa, Balloosh was

inhabited by ancient animals that once roamed in the wild long, long ago. Explore this happening habitat to take a step back into Jamaa's history.

PANDA

PANDAS ARE SOME OF THE WORLD'S MOST RECOGNIZABLE ANIMALS. Sporting white fur and distinctive black markings, they live in the wild only in mountainous bamboo forests in central China. Sadly, the forests they live in have been threatened by development, and, as a result, panda populations have dropped dramatically. But many people have been working hard to help pandas by establishing sanctuaries and breeding centers, and panda populations have begun to increase. In Jamaa, pandas are sometimes listed as endangered, meaning they are not always available for purchase. But you can always show off your panda pride by buying a panda topiary from the Topiary Shop in Sarepia Forest!

PANDAS HAVE FIVE FINGERS AND A THUMB-LIKE APPENDAGE THAT THEY USE ONLY FOR HOLDING BAMBOO.

PANDA CUBS EAT THEIR MOM'S POOP!

PANDA PIGMENT

Is there a special reason for pandas' black-and-white fur? Researchers think their white fur camouflages them in their snowy habitats, while the black fur on their legs and shoulders gives them cover in shady environments. The black markings around their eyes may help them recognize their fellow pandas.

Kangaroo

AJ Stats

INSPIRED BY: Red kangaroo (*Macropus rufus*)

SIGNATURE MOVE: When it comes to hopping, kangaroos can't be beat. When they hop, they do a backflip!

INSIDER INFO: Kangaroos have their very own app from the creators of Animal Jam called AJ Jump that you can download on your mobile device.

ADVENTURE SECRET: Play The Great Escape and go through the kangaroos-only passage to earn a cool prize!

WANT TO BE THE HAPPIEST HOPPER IN JAMAA? Well, kangaroos might be just the animals for you! With their long muscular tails and giant hind feet, these cool creatures are built for jumping ... and jiving! If there was a best dancer contest, the roos would win every time. When Jamaa's kangaroos dance, they do a backward boogie, jump right into the air, and turn right around to keep the party going.

MALE KANGAROOS ARE CALLED BOOMERS, AND FEMALES ARE CALLED FLIERS.

KANGAROOS CAN LEAP UP TO 10 FEET (3 M) IN THE AIR AND DISTANCES UP TO 30 FEET (9 M).

JUMPING JOEYS

Jamaa's kangaroos have one big difference from those in Australia: Kangaroos in Animal Jam don't have pouches! Kangaroos are marsupials, meaning the females raise their young in furry pouches after they're born. Newborn joeys can be as small as a grain of rice, and they depend on mom for everything. The pouch serves as protection for these fragile babies and it's also where they feed on mom's milk. Joeys will be ready to hop on their own one day—just like the adorable pet joeys you might see jumping around Jamaa!

SAVANNA ANIMALS

MANY TYPES OF ANIMALS MAKE THESE GRASSY PLAINS OF THE WORLD THEIR HOME, including herbivores like elephants and rhinoceroses, carnivores like lions and hyenas, many types of birds, and lots of insects. Just like in the wild, the savanna animals of Jamaa are social butterflies. You might find them hanging out together at parties!

ELEPHANT

ARE YOU FRIENDLY AND SOCIAL? Sounds like you might like to become an elephant! Elephants are the largest land animals alive today, but they aren't all brawn: Not only do they have excellent memories, they also have a complicated social order and live in herds of up to 100 elephants. Don't be surprised if you find these brainy animals hanging out together in the Chamber of Knowledge!

AJ Stats

INSPIRED BY: African savanna elephant (*Loxodonta africana*)

SIGNATURE MOVE: When Jamaa elephants play, they flap their ears and fly low to the ground.

INSIDER INFO: When elephants put on certain items, they wear them on their trunks or tusks instead of on their heads or bodies! Try on lots of fabulous fashions to see these looks in action.

ADVENTURE SECRET: Check out the elephants-only passage in The Hive to get a prize!

HYENA

IT'S NO LAUGHING MATTER: Hyenas might be the most misunderstood of all Jamaa's animals. Sometimes known as scavengers and thieves, they are actually very smart and are excellent hunters. The hyenas in Jamaa look a little different than their counterparts in the wild: They have a bushy tail that is like striped hyenas', but their default pattern is that of spotted hyenas. It's like you're getting two cool hyenas in one!

AJ Stats

INSPIRED BY: Spotted hyena
(*Crocuta crocuta*)
SIGNATURE MOVE: When hyenas play they laugh so hard they fall down.
INSIDER INFO: When hyenas wear a Sword, Pirate Sword, or Golden Pirate Sword, they actually get two blades crisscrossed on their backs. Nobody's going to mess with those hyenas!

AJ Stats

INSPIRED BY: Southern giraffe
(*Giraffa giraffa*)
SIGNATURE MOVE: When giraffes sleep in Jamaa, they curl up their legs and stretch out their necks. Yawn!
INSIDER INFO: Giraffes are the only animals in Jamaa that can have a coat pattern with diamond like patches.

GIRAFFE

EVER WISHED YOU WERE TALL ENOUGH TO REACH THE TOP SHELF WITHOUT A BOOST? Then you should become a giraffe, the tallest animal in the world. As a giraffe in Jamaa, you'll hang out with lions and hyenas and other animals no real-life giraffe would dream of being buddies with. And although your long neck may not necessarily help you reach the highest treasures in Jamaa, you *can* spin on your head—a trick that every Jamaa giraffe was born to do!

RHINO

DO YOU CHARGE HEADFIRST INTO NEW SITUATIONS? You may have the makings of a rhino! Rhinos are mostly solitary animals, but the females are very protective moms; they are fierce about defending their calves and will fight to keep them safe. The rhinos of Jamaa are ready to have some fun, although they show a bit of their tough side when they play, stomping the ground and shaking their head side to side.

AJ Stats

INSPIRED BY: Black rhinoceros
(*Diceros bicornis*)
SIGNATURE MOVE: When rhinos dance, they alternate kicking out their right legs and then left legs. Get down, rhino!
INSIDER INFO: You might see some Jammers exploring Jamaa with a Rhino Helmet. It's a super-rare item that you can usually only get by trading with Jammers.

FARM ANIMALS

ANIMALS THAT HUMANS HAVE TAMED AND ADAPTED TO USE FOR FOOD, WORK, AND PLAY ARE CONSIDERED "DOMESTICATED." Pets like dogs and cats are domesticated, and farm animals including horses, pigs, and cows are, too. Unlike wild animals, domesticated animals can't successfully live out in the world on their own; they rely on humans to survive. But in the lands of Jamaa, farm animals can explore alongside the wild animals. Jamaa even has a special den just for them—the Ol' Barn. It makes the perfect home for horses, pigs, llamas, sheep, and goats!

SHEEP

COUNTING REAL SHEEP BEFORE BED MAY HELP SOOTHE YOU TO SLEEP, but counting Jamaa's sheep might get you up and about instead! These small, fluffy critters hop instead of walk on their tiny stub feet. In the wild, sheep prefer to walk, of course, often in large groups called flocks. A flock of 1,300 sheep once got loose in Huesca, Spain, and walked through the city in the middle of the night!

AJ Stats

INSPIRED BY: Domestic sheep *(Ovis aries)*
SIGNATURE MOVE: Jamaa's sheep show their wild side when they play, jumping back and forth over a wooden fence.
INSIDER INFO: The discovery of Jamaa's sheep and their Heartstone is an important part of The Phantom Fortress.
ADVENTURE SECRET: Head through the sheep passage in The Phantom Fortress to nab a Sheep Hat.
ONLY IN PLAY WILD: Make sure to visit the sheep-only party and dance with the flock!

AJ Stats

INSPIRED BY: Domestic goat *(Capra aegagrus hircus)*
SIGNATURE MOVE: Have you ever seen a goat tap-dance? You will in Jamaa!
INSIDER INFO: Take the quiz in the goat minibook to win a shiny Goat Trophy!
ONLY IN PLAY WILD: When these hearty animals play, they go head-to-head against a steadfast barrel!

GOAT

LIKE TO TAKE THINGS UP A NOTCH? You might make a perfect goat. Goats are known for their great climbing abilities ... some can even climb trees! The goats in Jamaa like to aim higher, too: When hopping, they bounce up and down and do flips on a trampoline.

PIG

PIGS ... DIRTY? HOGWASH! These oinkers are known for getting muddy, but they roll in mud mostly to keep themselves cool. (They don't have working sweat glands.) Of course, the pigs in Jamaa have awfully nice dens, but they still love to lounge in a mud puddle when they play. Whether you are a standard pink pig or choose a more unusual pig color (purple, anyone?), don't forget to adopt yourself a pet piglet to bob alongside you!

AJ Stats

INSPIRED BY: Domestic pig *(Sus scrofa domesticus)*
SIGNATURE MOVE: Pigs in Jamaa are known for their dance moves. They slide left, then right, then hop and spin.
INSIDER INFO: Are you crazy about pigs? They're the only animal available in the Diamond Shop to all Jammers, both members and nonmembers!

FARM ANIMALS

LLAMA

DO YOU STUFF YOUR BACKPACK FULL and easily climb the stairs at school? You may be a llama in training. Llamas are able to carry up to 75 pounds (34 kg) for up to 20 miles (32 km)! If carrying heavy stuff isn't your thing, don't worry: Overburdened llamas often just lie down and refuse to move. Maybe that's why llamas in Jamaa look so snug with their legs tucked under them when they're sleeping!

AJ Stats

INSPIRED BY: Llama (*Lama glama*)

SIGNATURE MOVE: When llamas in Jamaa play, they prance in a circle.

INSIDER INFO: A carved image of a llama can be found above the entrance to the Canyons Pathway, located between Coral Canyons and Crystal Sands!

AJ Stats

INSPIRED BY: Horse (*Equus caballus*)

SIGNATURE MOVE: When horses play, they turn in a circle, jumping and kicking.

INSIDER INFO: Horses are one of only two animals that can have a stripe pattern.

ADVENTURE SECRET: Play through The Hive in Hard Mode and go through the horses-only passage.

ONLY IN PLAY WILD: Hang out in Horse Haven, found via a rainbow horses-only passage in the Canyons Pathway near Coral Canyons.

HORSE

ARE YOU A SUPERFAST RUNNER? Sounds like you might want to sprint into Jamaa as a horse! Horses in the wild can gallop up to 30 miles an hour (48 km/h)! In Jamaa, horses can show off their swiftness at the Jamaa Derby, the fun racing game where they are the only animals that can participate. Horses are grazing animals, so you won't be surprised to see them also hanging out as a herd in the grasslands of Appondale.

CLYDESDALE HORSE

ARE YOU ALWAYS WILLING TO LEND A HOOF? You may have the heart of a Clydesdale horse! These equines are what's known as draft horses, and have been used by people for hundreds of years to pull heavy loads—up to one ton (0.9 t)! Clydesdale horses are built tough: most tower taller than an adult human and can weigh up to 2,400 pounds (1,088 kg). That super strength should come in handy when taking on the Phantoms in Jamaa!

AJ Stats

INSPIRED BY: Clydesdale horse (*Equus caballus*)

SIGNATURE MOVE: Hop into a rocket ship and blast off with their otherworldly play move!

INSIDER INFO: Hoof it on over to the farm-themed Horses Only Party to hang out with all your fellow equines!

BOTH MALE AND FEMALE LEMURS ARE ABOUT THE SAME SIZE: 1.5 FEET (0.5 M) LONG AND ABOUT 5 POUNDS (2.3 KG).

AJ stats

INSPIRED BY:
Ring-tailed lemur
(*Lemur catta*)

SIGNATURE MOVE: The lemurs of Jamaa just love to spin, whether they are spinning themselves into a tornado when they play or hopping and spinning when they dance.

INSIDER INFO: Finish the quiz at the end of the lemur minibook, found in the first level of the Chamber of Knowledge in the Lost Temple of Zios, and you can win a Lemur Trophy.

ONLY IN PLAY WILD: Visit the top secret Lemur Lounge in Sarepia Forest!

ARE YOU LIKE A TORNADO BLOWING THROUGH THE HOUSE FULL OF WILD ENERGY? Well, you will find a friend in the lemurs of Jamaa! When they play, they turn themselves into dizzy, spinning balls, and all that can be seen are their colors. In the wild, there are more than 100 species of lemurs, and their energy levels vary. Some lemurs slow down to a sort of hibernation for anywhere from a few days to several months a year. Real ring-tailed lemurs love to chase, play-bite, jump on, and wrestle with other lemurs! Lucky for you, there are no biting lemurs in Jamaa, so you can focus your energy on defeating Phantoms.

SAVING LEMURS

Ring-tailed lemurs in the wild are very social creatures, living in groups of up to 17 members in the dry forest and bush of southern Madagascar. Because their forests are threatened, these petite primates are very endangered in the wild. Through breeding, education, and research, lemur conservation organizations are working to protect their habitat and increase their numbers.

LEMURS EAT LEAVES, FLOWERS, BARK, SAP, FRUIT, AS WELL AS INSECTS AND SMALL VERTEBRATES, SUCH AS CHAMELEONS.

27

CROCODILE

AJ Stats

INSPIRED BY:
Nile crocodile (*Crocodylus niloticus*)

SIGNATURE MOVE: Show off your moves! It's only appropriate that Nile crocodiles would groove to moves similar to the "Walk Like an Egyptian" dance popular in the 1980s.

INSIDER INFO: Crocodiles are one of only a handful of reptiles that live in the world of Jamaa.

DO YOU LIKE LOUNGING IN THE SUN OR HANGING OUT BY THE RIVER? You might consider becoming a mighty crocodile! Crocodiles are cold-blooded, which means they have to rely on sources outside their own body for heat. To warm up, they bask in the sun; to cool down again, they move into the shade or retreat under the water. So, lazing on the banks of the rivers of Jamaa comes naturally to them. For crocs, this isn't being lazy, it's "thermoregulating"! Pretty cool!

CROCODILES AND THEIR ANCESTORS HAVE BEEN AROUND FOR HUNDREDS OF MILLIONS OF YEARS—EVEN SURVIVING THE EXTINCTION EVENT THAT KILLED OFF THE DINOSAURS.

OPEN WIDE

My, what big teeth you have! Crocodiles use their giant mouths for more than just chowing down. Crocs can't sweat, so they open up and do something called "mouth gaping" to beat the heat. And when croc babies hatch, moms look like they're getting ready for dinner! But instead, they head over to the nest and carry their new offspring to the riverbank in their mouths—releasing them to their new watery world.

Deer

AJ Stats

INSPIRED BY: White-tailed deer
(*Odocoileus virginianus*)

SIGNATURE MOVE: When the deer of
Jamaa dance, they show off the
species' natural grace by prancing
backward and then leaping.

INSIDER INFO: Deer have a special
spot pattern that goes all over
the neck to the back, just like a
wild deer.

ONLY IN PLAY WILD: When deer visit
Mt. Shiveer, they'll find a deer-only
passage leading to Deer Highlands.
There, they can scamper around
with other fleet-footed does and
bucks and buy some awesome deer
gear at the Deer Highlands Shop.

DEER ARE "CREPUSCULAR," MEANING THEY'RE MOST ACTIVE AT DAWN AND DUSK.

ARE YOU ALERT AND QUICK, READY TO LEAP AWAY FROM DANGER IN A SINGLE BOUND? You might have the makings of an agile deer. In nature, deer have lots of predators, so they are naturally shy; deer in Jamaa aren't so different. They might look relaxed, but they'll spring up ready to run when they play. In the wild only male deer have antlers—and those are shed and regrown every year—but in Jamaa you can wear antlers proudly all year long, whether you are a boy or a girl!

BABY DEER, CALLED FAWNS, HAVE REDDISH BROWN FUR WITH WHITE SPOTS THAT HELPS CAMOUFLAGE THEM IN THE FOREST.

Delightful Deer

White-tailed deer get their name from the white underside of their tail. While they're mostly found in forested or grassy meadow areas of North and Central America, their habitat also extends into cities and other populated areas. It's not uncommon to find white-tailed deer in suburban backyards—especially yards with tasty vegetable gardens!

29

AWESOME
ARBOREAL ANIMALS

LIKE A GOOD VIEW? Some of Jamaa's most interesting animals prefer to spend more time in trees than on the ground. Called arboreal animals, they include red pandas, monkeys, sloths, and koalas. In the wild, these cool creatures spend the majority of their time hanging from tree branches. They eat, sleep, and hang out with other animals—all in the leaves of the canopy! Although every animal in Jamaa can climb and play in the giant acacia tree in Appondale, arboreal animals may especially love spending time here.

KOALA

IN THE WILD, KOALAS ARE FOUND IN EUCALYPTUS FORESTS IN AUSTRALIA, where they play, sleep, and eat, snacking on eucalyptus leaves. They generally only leave the safety of the tree branches to move from one tree to another. With their fuzzy fur, huge furry brown ears, and oversize noses, they are beloved by many Jammers. They're often off traveling, so be sure to become one when you see they're available. The last time they returned from their travels, they brought home news of a new land: Kimbara Outback!

AJ Stats

INSPIRED BY: Koala (*Phascolarctos cinereus*)
ALPHA: Cosmo
SIGNATURE MOVE: The koalas of Jamaa really know how to hula!
INSIDER INFO: The Koala Topiary may be crazy cool, but during the Jamaalidays, look out for the festive version—the Lit Koala Topiary.
ADVENTURE SECRET: There is a koalas-only passage in the last cave near the end of the adventure Meet Cosmo.
ONLY IN PLAY WILD: Check out the koala e-book in the Chamber of Knowledge and complete the quiz to win a Koala Trophy!

SLOTH

IF YOU DON'T MIND TAKING YOUR TIME, SLOTHS MAY JUST BE THE ANIMALS FOR YOU. Sloths are among the slowest creatures on the planet—so slow it takes them up to a month just to digest one meal! Although in the wild they're as chill as you can get, sloths in Jamaa are up for all the action. You'll probably find them hanging out in the trees or the river in the Lost Temple of Zios or with their fellow tree dwellers at the Paradise Party.

AJ Stats

INSPIRED BY: Brown-throated three-toed sloth (*Bradypus variegatus*)

SIGNATURE MOVE: In true sloth form, sloths play by hanging upside down and spinning around.

INSIDER INFO: Take the quiz at the end of the sloth minibook in the Chamber of Knowledge to receive your very own Sloth Trophy! Slow-motion high-five!

AJ Stats

INSPIRED BY: Variegated spider monkey (*Ateles hybridus*)

ALPHA: Graham

SIGNATURE MOVE: Monkeys like to do the robot dance.

INSIDER INFO: Head to the Monkeys Only Party to listen to Monkey Madness on repeat, buy monkey items, and explore the branches of a giant tree.

ADVENTURE SECRET: Look out for the monkeys-only cave entrance in The Great Escape.

ONLY IN PLAY WILD: Visit the Monkey Kingdom, located through the monkey passage in Sarepia Forest.

MONKEY

ARE YOU A CHAMP ON THE JUNGLE GYM? Sounds like you'd have a swinging good time monkeying around in Jamaa! You'll find monkeys anywhere in the world there's a heavy canopy of treetops for them to swing back and forth between. So it'll be no surprise to see monkeys hanging out in leafy playgrounds of Sarepia Forest or the Lost Temple of Zios. Curious and playful, monkeys fit right into Jamaa, where there's always tons to learn and fun to be had.

RED PANDA

THOUGH THEY'RE NOT CLOSELY RELATED TO THEIR MORE WELL-KNOWN COUSINS, the fluffy, ruddy-colored animals with long bushy tails do share giant pandas' love of bamboo. Both pandas are from Asia, but red pandas spend most of their time in trees. So it shouldn't be a surprise to see these mostly solitary mammals hanging out in the treetops in Sarepia Forest and the Lost Temple of Zios!

AJ Stats

INSPIRED BY: Red panda (*Ailurus fulgens*)

SIGNATURE MOVE: These agile animals dance on one paw and with a giant leap into the air, flip over gracefully, ending with a perfect landing!

INSIDER INFO: Earn a Red Panda Plushie by completing the Journey Book page for Mt. Shiveer.

ONLY IN PLAY WILD: Get the Mystical Fortress, which features sweeping mountain views—it's the perfect den to make these alpine-dwelling animals feel right at home!

PreHistoric PreDators

HUNDREDS OF THOUSANDS OF YEARS AGO, many of the wild animals that roamed Earth were quite different from today's species. In fact, most of today's mammals might be considered tame compared to the fierce predators of the past! But in Jamaa, don't be surprised to see an ancient animal or two exploring alongside you!

DireWolf

AJ Stats

INSPIRED BY: Dire wolf *(Canis dirus)*
SIGNATURE MOVE: Just like their smaller canine cousins, Jamaa's direwolves are obsessed with finding and burying bones when they play!
INSIDER INFO: Direwolves can attend the Wolves Only Party and boogie down with their wolf and arctic wolf buddies.

A MuCH LarGer WOLF

Averaging 130 pounds (59 kg), dire wolves were more than 40 pounds (18 kg) heavier than today's gray wolves. In fact, many Ice Age animals were downright enormous by today's standards. But why? Scientists think part of the reason may have been to help them catch dinner! As herbivores grew larger (likely to digest plants better), predators like dire wolves needed to keep up to keep munching.

DO YOU WANT TO BECOME A BIGGER, badder wolf than all the rest? Then try going prehistoric and journey through Jamaa as a direwolf! Though these bygone creatures have been lost to history, scientists have been able to learn a lot about them by studying their fossils. Ancient wolves lived in the ancient Americas during the Ice Age, from what's today Alberta, Canada, to Bolivia in South America. They were slightly larger and had a more powerful bite than their modern gray wolf cousins. Looking to join a wolf pack in Jamaa? Just like today's wild wolves, prehistoric wolves also hunted in packs. So, never fear, Jamaa's direwolves will feel right at home with a pack full of wolves of all shapes and sizes!

DIRE WOLVES MYSTERIOUSLY DISAPPEARED ABOUT 10,000 YEARS AGO; SCIENTISTS AREN'T SURE WHY.

AJ Stats

INSPIRED BY: Saber-toothed cat (*Smilodon fatalis*)

SIGNATURE MOVE: Unlike many other animals in Jamaa, saber-tooths don't run when they move. Instead, they silently stalk from place to place.

INSIDER INFO: Sabertooths were the first ancient animals to come to Jamaa. Their Heartstone was discovered in the ruins of a sunken city in the fun Adventure, The Mystery Below.

Small Hunters, Big Teeth

Say cheese! *Smilodon* had deadly sharp, serrated canines that grew up to seven inches (18 cm) long. But just how useful were these chompers when hunting? It was possible for their teeth to break if they bent the wrong way. Because of this, many scientists think that *Smilodon*'s jagged canines were actually used to deliver precise, fatal stab wounds while they had their prey pinned. Now that's not a smile you'd want to see!

ARE LIONS, TIGERS, OR OTHER MODERN-DAY wild cats too tame for your taste? You may want to become one of the fiercest felines in Jamaa: sabertooths. These distant cat relatives stalked the Earth between 11,000 and 40,000 years ago, roaring and brandishing their impressive canine teeth. Called *Smilodon* by scientists, they were about a foot (30 cm) shorter than today's lions but twice as heavy, and had a stubby tail. Scientists think that because of these features, *Smilodon* probably didn't hunt prey across long distances, instead waiting patiently to ambush a potential meal. Though most of today's wild cats, such as tigers, leopards, and cougars, are solitary animals, paleontologists believe saber-toothed cats lived in prides, just like lions today. That's good news for social Jammers looking to roam Jamaa with a pride of their own!

SMILODON FATALIS IS CALIFORNIA, U.S.A.'S STATE FOSSIL.

COOL CANINES

WHEN YOU HEAR PEOPLE TALKING ABOUT CANINES, THEY OFTEN MEAN DOGS. But did you know the family Canidae actually contains dozens of species of dogs, wolves, foxes, jackals, and other animals? The foxes, wolves, and coyotes of Jamaa are all equally awesome, so have fun partying throughout Jamaa as any or all of them!

COYOTE

IF YOU ARE CLEVER and perhaps a bit mischievous, coyotes are the animals for you. In folklore, coyotes are known as tricksters and, in real life, they are super adaptable. They can be found anywhere there is food—even in cities! It's no surprise then that coyotes can be found all over Jamaa, hanging with their canine pals.

AJ Stats

INSPIRED BY: Coyote *(Canis latrans)*
SIGNATURE MOVE: They chase their tails when they play!
INSIDER INFO: Coyotes look great wearing any other Wild West–themed items. Perfect for these desert-loving canines!

WOLF

IF YOU CONSIDER YOURSELF SOCIAL, then you should become a wolf! Wolves live in packs, which are families of up to 20 wolves that live and hunt together. There are plenty of other Jammers to form a pack with, because members and nonmembers alike can become a wolf.

AJ Stats

INSPIRED BY: Gray wolf *(Canis lupus)*
ALPHA: Greely
SIGNATURE MOVE: When wolves dance, they do the twist!
INSIDER INFO: Pick up a Wolf Totem at the Wolves Only Party!
ADVENTURE SECRET: Wolves are just one of a few animals that can explore The Hidden Falls.
ONLY IN PLAY WILD: Have a howling good time at the Wolf Cave—the ultimate hangout space for wolves and arctic wolves!

ArCtic FOX

ARE YOU CLEVER AND RESOURCEFUL? Arctic foxes live in some of the coldest places on Earth and have adapted to find food in some unlikely ways. They stock up on snacks during the "warm" seasons, eating berries, bird eggs, fish, and more. In the winter, they use their amazing hearing to find prey beneath the snow. They listen closely, and then dive into the snow to get to mice or voles. When the arctic foxes in Jamaa play, they chase a mouse into a hole—just as they would in the wild.

AJ StatS

INSPIRED BY: Arctic fox (*Vulpes lagopus*)
SIGNATURE MOVE: When they dance, they stand on their hind legs and wave their front legs in the air!
INSIDER INFO: Once you select another fur color as an arctic fox, you can't go back to the default.
ADVENTURE SECRET: The Phantom Badlands has two passages that only arctic foxes can enter.

AJ StatS

INSPIRED BY: Arctic wolf (*Canis lupus arctos*)
SIGNATURE MOVE: They sit like a wolf but roll around on the floor like a dog.
INSIDER INFO: Adopt a pet arctic wolf and travel around Jamaa in your very own pack.
ADVENTURE SECRET: Arctic wolves can open secret entrances in Return of the Phantoms, The Hidden Falls, and The Phantom Fortress.
ONLY IN PLAY WILD: Play with at least two other wolves in the Arctic Wolf Ice Cave on Mt. Shiveer and a giant smoke arctic wolf might appear!

ArCtic WOLF

DON'T BE FOOLED BY THEIR ELEGANT WHITE FUR. These icy individuals are just as fierce as their wolf cousins. Arctic wolves are actually a subspecies of the gray wolf, though they are slightly smaller in size. Feeling a little small? Don't worry. Head to Jamaa Township's Diamond Shop and check out the giant arctic wolf statue that will stop you in your tracks.

FOX

IF YOU'RE THE TYPE TO SAVE YOUR CANDY FOR A RAINY DAY, you and foxes may have a lot in common. Foxes often store food in their den to eat later, sometimes not coming back to it for months ... or ever! In the wild and in Jamaa, foxes really like being underground. When Jamaa foxes play, they dig a hole and then pop out the other side!

AJ StatS

INSPIRED BY: Red fox (*Vulpes vulpes*)
SIGNATURE MOVE: When foxes hop, they wave their bushy tails in the air.
INSIDER INFO: Watch the "It Wasn't Me" video in the Appondale Theater to see foxes in a starring role.
ADVENTURE SECRET: There's a foxes-only passage in The Phantom Portal.
ONLY IN PLAY WILD: To find the Fox Lair, a secret hangout for foxes and arctic foxes, search Appondale for a dark cave marked by a fox head.

BUNNY

RABBITS HAVE NEARLY 360-DEGREE VISION, WHICH MEANS THEY CAN SEE IN ALMOST ALL DIRECTIONS AT THE SAME TIME.

AJ Stats

INSPIRED BY: Eastern cottontail rabbit (*Sylvilagus floridanus*)

ALPHA: Peck

SIGNATURE MOVE: Bunnies in Jamaa break-dance, spinning on the tips of their ears.

INSIDER INFO: Jamaa's bunnies have their very own app! It's called Tunnel Town, and you can download it on your mobile device.

ADVENTURE SECRET: A Bunny Statue is one of the prizes available for Jammers who complete Return of the Phantoms.

ONLY IN PLAY WILD: The Bunny Burrow is just a hop, skip, and a jump through the Lost Temple of Zios. Look for a rabbit hole next to a tiki bunny!

BUNNIES ARE SOME OF THE SMALLEST AND MOST ADORABLE ANIMALS IN ALL OF JAMAA! With one ear drooping, they look especially sweet when they sleep. But when it comes time to play, they're all business—with their ears whipping so fast they launch right into the air! Although real-life rabbits may not take off like a helicopter, their ears are super important: They help them to hear predators. Being small, they're vulnerable to a lot of other animals, so they need to have great hearing and be superquick to stay safe. When fleeing a predator, they hop away in a zigzag pattern.

Wacky Warrens

Wild rabbits are mostly nocturnal, living underground in burrows or networks of burrows called warrens (kind of like Bunny Burrow in Return of the Phantoms, the first Adventure!). Though bunnies venture out near the warren to graze and feed, wild rabbits also enjoy a leisurely meal in their subterranean homes: They pass undigested food into soft droppings and then eat it again!

RABBITS CAN HOP UP TO 18 MILES AN HOUR (29 KM/H)!

36

RACCOON

AJ Stats

INSPIRED BY: North American raccoon *(Procyon lotor)*

SIGNATURE MOVE: The raccoons in Jamaa love an Irish jig.

INSIDER INFO: When the Summer Carnival is in town, you can get a Raccoon Tail! Complete the look by heading to Epic Wonders in Coral Canyons and buying a Raccoon Hat.

ADVENTURE SECRET: Don't miss the raccoons-only passage located in the final cave in Meet Cosmo.

ONLY IN PLAY WILD: Raccoons love to relax in the Raccoon River, the special raccoons-only area found in the Lost Temple of Zios.

Handy Adaptation

Raccoons have very special front paws, which they use like hands to hold food, fish, and even open jars! Although they use their paws like hands, they don't have thumbs, so they are not really like the hands of humans or monkeys. Instead, they use their long middle digits to come together with the two digits on either side of the paw, which allows them to grasp things.

ADAPTABLE RACCOONS LIVE BOTH IN THE CITY AND THE COUNTRY, drawn to wherever food is plentiful. These clever creatures are often known as bandits, and not just for the black mask around their eyes! They are super smart and pretty sneaky, finding food wherever they can (including your trash can or dog's bowl). Raccoons in the wild make a lot of noises, growling when they're threatened, purring when they are content, and chittering to each other. So it's no surprise that Jamaa's raccoons sit back and laugh when they play! If you like to play Animal Jam at night, that's the perfect time to roam Jamaa as a raccoon. Raccoons in the wild are nocturnal, meaning they do their playing, exploring, and eating during the night—saving their sleep for daylight hours.

ALTHOUGH RACCOONS DON'T ACTUALLY HIBERNATE, THEY SLEEP LONGER DURING WINTER THAN DURING OTHER PARTS OF THE YEAR.

WiLD Cats

THERE ARE 38 SPECIES OF WILD CATS—including lions, tigers, jaguars, leopards, and more—and some scientists think there might be more they don't know about yet! Wild cats are found in almost every habitat, so you'll definitely see them all over Jamaa. So let out a roar, meow, or purr and get ready to learn secrets about Jamaa's fantastic felines.

Tiger

IF YOU'RE A CAT LOVER, chances are you'll want to explore Jamaa as a tiger. Wild tigers are the largest cats in the world, and they love to swim! So don't be surprised to see them hanging out in the rivers of Jamaa. Tigers were the first animals in Jamaa to have their own original pattern: stripes, of course! You can change their pattern if you like: Some say tigers can't change their stripes, but they've clearly never been to Jamaa!

AJ Stats

INSPIRED BY: Siberian tiger (*Panthera tigris altaica*)

ALPHA: Sir Gilbert

SIGNATURE MOVE: When tigers dance, they can't help turning cartwheels.

INSIDER INFO: Big or small? How about both?! Get a Tiger Plushie and a Giant Tiger Plushie for your den.

ADVENTURE SECRET: Enter the tigers-only passage in The Phantom Fortress to get a Tiger Stripe Rug for your den.

ONLY IN PLAY WILD: Tigers get the royal treatment when they visit Tiger Resort—accessed via a secret passageway in the flowers of Crystal Sands.

AJ Stats

INSPIRED BY: Cheetah (*Acinonyx jubatus*)

SIGNATURE MOVE: Cheetahs speed off-screen so fast they're a blur!

INSIDER INFO: Cheetahs have their own unique pattern—swirls!

CHEETAH

FEEL LIKE THE FASTEST and most furious feline in the lands as you charge across the savannas of Appondale! Cheetahs are the speediest land animals in the world. They can sprint up to 70 miles an hour (113 km/h)—as fast as a car speeding down a highway. Cheetahs in Jamaa may not be quicker than the other animals, but they do have a supercool dance. And real-life cheetahs can't stand on their back legs and then do splits!

LION

IF YOU'RE STRONG AND LOUD and your favorite thing to do is hang out with dozens of your best friends, you might want to consider exploring Jamaa as this cool cat. In the wild, lions are one of the few felines that enjoy being social. They live in groups called prides of up to 30 members; that's a big family! These kings and queens of the jungle have a royally good time hanging out with all their buddies in Jamaa!

AJ Stats

INSPIRED BY: African lion (*Panthera leo*)

SIGNATURE MOVE: Lions mean business even when they play. They stand up tall, stamp the ground, and roar!

INSIDER INFO: Adopt a pet lion and journey through Jamaa as your very own lion pride.

ADVENTURE SECRET: Sneak through the lions-only entrance in The Phantom Portal to get a purr-fect prize.

ONLY IN PLAY WILD: Regal lions can let their manes down when hanging out with their fellow felines in the Lion's Den. You can access it through a secret passage in Appondale.

WiLD Cats

SNOW LEOPARD

ARE YOU AT HOME IN THE COLD? Do you prefer to go it alone? Snow leopards are right there with you! Wild snow leopards spend much of their time solo in the icy, steep, snow-covered mountains of Central Asia. In fact, they spend so much of their time alone (and in hard-to-reach places), scientists have a hard time observing them. Though unlike in the wild, snow leopards in Jamaa love to be right in the center of the action. On any given day, you're sure to see tons of snow leopards exploring all the fun Jamaa has to offer.

AJ Stats

INSPIRED BY: Snow leopard (*Panthera uncia*)
SIGNATURE MOVE: Snow leopards never let their guard down; even when they sleep, their tails twitch.
INSIDER INFO: Pick up The Snow Leopard Claw and win your own adorable Snow Leopard Plushies!
ONLY IN PLAY WILD: Secretive snow leopards feel perfectly safe when visiting their private sanctuary on Mt. Shiveer, Snow Leopard Ridge.

AJ Stats

INSPIRED BY: Cougar (*Puma concolor*)
SIGNATURE MOVE: Cougars shimmy to the right and the left when they dance.
INSIDER INFO: Ace the quiz in the back of the cougar minibook in the Chamber of Knowledge to receive a Cougar Trophy.

COUGAR

IF YOU'RE ADAPTABLE, love exploring new places, and like to be on the move, you might be a cougar. In the wild, cougars can be found in a number of different habitats, including forests, swamps, deserts, and prairies. They'll also travel up to six miles (10 km) every night in search of food. Like the other big cats of Jamaa, cougars share some traits of domestic cats—playing around by chasing and pouncing on a laser pointer!

LYNX

LYNX ARE STEALTHY CREATURES WITH GREAT EYESIGHT. These forest dwellers emerge at night to hunt, so they are rarely seen. Like lynx in the wild, lynx in Jamaa have large feet and ears with tufts. The tufts of hair at their ears help them hear prey, while wide paws act like built-in snowshoes. When they hop around in Jamaa, the fluffy tips of their ears point downward.

AJ Stats

INSPIRED BY: Bobcat (*Lynx rufus*)
SIGNATURE MOVE: Lynx like to play with balls of yarn—kind of like your kitty at home!
INSIDER INFO: Lynx have a special stripes-and-spots pattern that no other animals have.
ONLY IN PLAY WILD: As a lynx, you can choose a cool cat eye to complete your purr-fect look.

SAVING WILD CATS

Despite being smart, strong, and sometimes solitary creatures, many cats are vulnerable, threatened, or endangered in the wild. There are many reasons why these powerful cats are under attack. They suffer from the same issues that many other animals do—threats to their habitat due to human encroachment, poaching, and climate change. Of course, Jammers want safety for all animals, so visit the Conservation Museum in Appondale to find out how you can help. You can even donate gems toward the conservation of lions, tigers, or cheetahs!

PLAY WILD ANIMALS

DO YOU TAKE JAMAA WITH YOU ON THE GO? The mobile version of Animal Jam has some awesome animals that are only available on your mobile device. So go ahead, get comfy anywhere you are, and try becoming one of these special species!

ARABIAN HORSE

DO YOU LIKE TO GET A LITTLE FANCY? These elegant equines are often described as one of the most majestic horse breeds. It's no wonder, since throughout history Arabian horses carried kings, generals, and even starred in movies! But while they might be classy creatures, Arabian horses were originally kept by nomads who lived in the harsh deserts of the Arabian Peninsula where only the strong succeed. So, while you might decide to sport a stylish look as an Arabian horse in Jamaa, you'll definitely be one of the toughest animals battling the Phantoms.

U.S. PRESIDENT GEORGE WASHINGTON HAD AN ARABIAN STALLION NAMED MAGNOLIA.

SUPER STAMINA

Today, Arabian horses dominate in endurance sports. They are said to be one of the best breeds for distance riding. Around the world, horses and riders compete in long races—sometimes up to 100 miles (160 km)! During these races, horses are checked by veterinarians after every lap of the course to make sure they are fit to keep riding, and only the toughest are cleared to continue. In many races, only about 40 percent of horses complete the full course.

42

KOMODO DRAGONS HAVE 60 TEETH, BUT THEY'RE FOR SLICING AND TEARING—NOT CHEWING. THESE LIZARDS SWALLOW CHUNKS OF FOOD WHOLE!

BEING KING MIGHT SOUND LIKE TOUGH WORK, but fortunately, if you become a Komodo dragon—the reigning ruler of all wild lizards—in Jamaa, the toughest decision you'll have to make is which awesome expedition to go on next! Komodo dragons are the largest living lizards on Earth and can grow up to 10 feet (3 m) long and weigh more than 300 pounds (136 kg)! Scientists are also hard at work studying these monitors' monstrous maws—they contain a toxic venom that helps take down prey. Fortunately for those who dare to become dragons in Jamaa, the only fearsome fate you'll need to worry about is another dragon sticking its tongue out at you while they play!

AJ stats

INSPIRED BY: Komodo dragon (*Varanus komodoensis*)

SIGNATURE MOVE: These lovable lizards jump up on two scaly feet, jump and jive from side to side, and clap, starting the marvelous move all over again!

INSIDER INFO: While the Ancient Dragon Outfit looks cool on all of Jamaa's animals, it was custom-built to look fierce on Komodo dragons.

DESPITE THEIR SIZE, KOMODO DRAGONS' BITES ARE WEAKER THAN HOUSE CATS' BITES.

SUN'S OUT, TONGUES OUT

Did that Komodo dragon just stick its tongue out at you? Don't worry, he's not being rude—that's how lizards smell! Just like their not-so-distant relatives, snakes, lizards used their forked tongues to catch scents. When Komodos stick out their tongues, they're able to collect scent particles and pull them back into their mouths. Then they press their tongues to the roof of their mouths, where they have special cells that can detect the scent. So, give lizards a pass—they're just making sense of all the scents.

Meet the
OCEAN ANIMALS

Slide into the sea as a penguin, float freely on the surface of the waves as an otter, and even dive deep into the ocean depths as a dolphin! In the wild, oceans cover more than 70 percent of the planet's surface, and are filled with all kinds of incredible creatures. While some ocean animals in Jamaa, such as sea turtles, sharks, dolphins, and octopuses, can only explore underwater, other animals, such as penguins, seals, otters, and polar bears can explore the world both above and below the sea. Dive in!

EXPLORE THE OCEANS OF JAMAA

Bahari Bay

Kani Cove

Deep Blue

Crystal Reef

INSIDER INFO

OCEAN DWELLERS HAVE THEIR VERY OWN OCEAN ADVENTURE BASE CAMP! You can reach it from Bahari Bay or through the Adventure Base Camp.

BAHARI BAY

This ocean is the gateway to the sea, and is the first place Jammers should visit when they become their first ocean animal. The bay is full of beautiful ocean plants, coral, and green-blue water, similar to the warm-water ocean homes of many tropical species. From here you can swim on to Ocean Adventure Base Camp or dive deeper to different oceans.

DEEP BLUE

Deep Blue is the darkest, deepest ocean in Jamaa. The Earth's ocean depths are cold and dark, home to anglerfish, sixgill sharks, and giant spider crabs. In Jamaa, you may swim by these and other marine animals that live only in the darkest part of the sea.

CRYSTAL REEF

Crystal Reef is full of bright and colorful corals. In the wild, coral reefs are the backbone of marine life in many parts of the world and thrive in shallow, warm water. In Jamaa, this is where you'll find Flippers 'N Fins, the ocean pet shop, as well as some of the most brightly colored tropical fish species. Crystal Reef connects to all the other oceans except Kani Cove.

KANI COVE

The world's shoreline is made up of many inlets, coves, bays, and fjords—places where land meets water. So in Jamaa, it's no surprise this cool cove connects to the land above—and that there's so much to discover! It's the perfect place for lost treasure and even has a sunken shipwreck. You can connect to Tierney's Aquarium from Kani Cove or stay an ocean animal and swim over to Deep Blue.

SHARK

ARE YOU THE FIRST ONE IN YOUR HOUSE TO SMELL DINNER COOKING? Your superb sniffer would make you a swimmingly good shark! Great whites can smell blood from miles away, and the part of sharks' brains that is dedicated to smell is large compared with that in other animals. Sharks are apex predators—meaning they are at the top of the ocean food chain. Their presence not only helps keep a good balance of ocean life, but their health also helps scientists determine the health of the whole ocean. Sharks are an important part of life in Jamaa, and can be found in every ocean. If you like exploring the water and sniffing around for adventure, flash a toothy grin and enter Jamaa as a shark!

> THERE ARE MORE THAN 465 SPECIES OF SHARKS!

> A GROUP OF SHARKS IS CALLED A SHIVER.

ON THE MOVE

Like other fish, sharks use their gills to breathe underwater. They absorb oxygen from water when the water moves over their gills. Some species swim through the water to ventilate their gills (ram ventilation), while others pump water over their gills (called buccal pumping). Most sharks can do both, but some can't do buccal pumping. They have to keep moving or they'll drown!

AJ Stats

INSPIRED BY: Green sea turtle *(Chelonia mydas)*

SIGNATURE MOVE: Jamaa's sea turtles swirl and dive while under the waves!

INSIDER INFO: The pet turtles of Jamaa can follow you on land and into the ocean!

ADVENTURE SECRET: Play Bubble Trouble in Hard Mode to discover the sea turtles-only passage!

ARE YOU THE LIFE OF THE PARTY? Do you come out of your shell easily? You may want to swim gracefully into Jamaa as a sea turtle! When Jamaa's sea turtles dance, they take off their shells and wear them like hats, and when they play, they take off their shells and throw them in the air! In nature, sea turtles' outer shells are called carapaces, and they're made up of keratin (like your hair and fingernails) and bones. (And, unlike sea turtle shells in Jamaa, they don't come off!) These strong shells have many functions—but their most important job is providing protection from predators.

EGG-CELLENT ADVENTURE

Although sea turtles live most of their lives in the water, they come on to land to lay their eggs. The mother sea turtle returns to the water after burying the eggs, and about two months later, the eggs hatch. The hatchlings must make their slow way back down the beach to the water. Their journey leaves them vulnerable to predators, so many countries now have sea turtle programs where they protect the eggs before they hatch and then shepherd the hatchlings to the relative safety of the sea.

SEA TURTLES HAVE EXISTED FOR 110 MILLION YEARS, MEANING THEIR ANCESTORS WERE ALIVE WHEN THERE WERE DINOSAURS.

A SEA TURTLE CAN WEIGH AS MUCH AS A WATER BUFFALO!

OCTOPUS

AJ Stats

INSPIRED BY: Giant Pacific octopus (*Enteroctopus dofleini*)
SIGNATURE MOVE: The octopuses in Jamaa use their tentacles to jump rope!
INSIDER INFO: Octopuses are the only invertebrates in Jamaa!

ARE YOU BIGHEARTED AND SUPER SMART? That means you have a lot in common with octopuses! Octopuses have three hearts and nine brains—all located in their limbs! (Well, maybe you're not *that* similar to octopuses.) If you've seen these astonishing eight-armed animals swimming around Jamaa, you know how much fun it is to be an octopus. You wouldn't expect octopuses to dance like ballerinas, but they do in Jamaa. Although, considering that octopuses are invertebrates—meaning they don't have any bones—they *should* be pretty flexible!

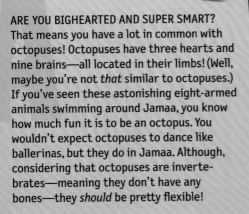

OCTOPUSES CAN "SEE" WITH THEIR SKIN!

Super Suckers

When most people think of octopuses, they think of their signature suckers. Octopuses' eight arms can be covered in up to 2,000 suckers, each one capable of moving on its own. And they're super strong: Each has microscopic grooves, which aid in forming a seal, like a suction cup. All those suckers working together help octopuses grab and hold on to surfaces and prey. They also use their powerful arms to move rocks around to form their dens. Sometimes, octopuses will even use a rock for a "door," which they pull closed once inside!

AJ Stats

INSPIRED BY: Common bottlenose dolphin *(Tursiops truncatus)*

ALPHA: Tavie

SIGNATURE MOVE: Just like in the wild, Jamaa dolphins love to play by swimming vertically using only their tail flukes.

INSIDER INFO: Swim to Bahari Bay or the Sol Arcade to play Splash and Dash, where dolphins race to the finish! Keep playing to earn all nine achievements.

ADVENTURE SECRET: Free the Bottlenose Brigade and don't miss the possibility of winning a Brigade-themed item in Turning the Tide.

ARE YOU FRIENDLY AND PLAYFUL? Dolphins are, too, both in Jamaa and in nature. They love to dive through the waves and frolic with their dolphin buddies—they even somersault underwater! It's no surprise that you're bound to see tons of them as you explore the oceans of Jamaa.

DOLPHINS CAN HEAR SOUNDS UNDERWATER FROM 15 MILES (24 KM) AWAY.

DOLPHINS SLEEP WITH ONE EYE OPEN.

Marvelous Marine Mammals

Unlike most animals of the deep, dolphins are mammals. That means they give birth to live young and nurse their babies. Other traits they share with humans are a four-chambered heart and being warm-blooded (meaning they supply their own heat, unlike reptiles that need the sun to warm them). Although dolphins aren't critically endangered, most countries protect them from hunting and other threats.

LanD anD Sea

IF YOU'RE THE KIND OF PERSON WHO'S AS COMFORTABLE IN THE WATER AS YOU ARE OUT OF IT, THESE ANIMALS ARE YOUR JAM! In the wild and in Jamaa, they like to hang out on land and in the sea; they can spend time underwater, but they also can explore the land. These versatile creatures are the only animals in Jamaa who get access to the best of both worlds!

PenGUiN

ARE YOU SOCIAL AND A SNAZZY DRESSER? Then you have a lot in common with Jamaa's penguins. They are dignified and elegant—except, perhaps, when they're wobbling and spinning on one foot and then the other when they dance! In the wild, penguins live in Australia, New Zealand, the Galápagos, and even parts of South America and Africa, but scientists are especially worried about the penguins of Antarctica, who are losing their icy habitat due to climate change. When waddling through Jamaa as a penguin, be sure to read about all the ways you can help save these creatures and their home.

AJ STaTS

INSPIRED BY: Little penguin (*Eudyptula minor*)

SIGNATURE MOVE: In the water, penguins play by spinning in a circle while they blow bubbles.

INSIDER INFO: A penguin's belly color is a special white that isn't on the color palette. If you change it, you can't get it back!

ADVENTURE SECRET: Explore the penguins-only passage in Turning the Tide.

ONLY IN PLAY WILD: While there are no ocean worlds to explore on the mobile version of Animal Jam, penguins can still get their swim on—they do the backstroke through Jamaa's waters.

Polar Bear

IF *BRRRRR* DOESN'T BOTHER YOU, navigating Jamaa as a polar bear might be a cool choice for you. Polar bears live on the shore and ice floes, spending much of their time in the sea. They swim to survive—pursuing seals, their prey of choice—in and out of water. Polar bears are as vulnerable as their habitat, the Arctic ice. Sometimes the polar bears of Jamaa are traveling or endangered, but when they come back, you can have tons of fun as a polar bear!

Otter

IF YOU'D LOVE NOTHING MORE THAN TO SPEND YOUR SUMMER FLOATING IN A POOL, you might be destined for the life of an otter! You can often find otters floating on their backs, usually with a group of other otters. (Sometimes they anchor themselves to a spot by wrapping kelp around their bodies.) They can do almost anything while comfortably floating, including eating dinner and taking care of their babies.

Seal

SEALS ENJOY DIVING DEEP UNDER THE WAVES IN THEIR HUNT FOR FISH, but they also love catching some rays at the surface; you can sometimes see groups of hundreds of them sunbathing together. If this chill scene sounds like something you could warm up to, you might want to jump into Jamaa as a seal! When summer hits in Jamaa, score the Water Park and host your own sunbathing den party with as many Jammers as you can gather.

Meet the
FLYiNG ANiMALS

Want a bird's-eye view of Jamaa? Swoop in as one of its flying animals. Flying animals in Jamaa can do one thing that birds in the wild can't—dance! Flying animals in the wild play, but they probably don't purposefully make themselves dizzy like the owls of Jamaa, or stop midair and make the clouds their own personal dance floor like falcons! Get ready to spread your wings and meet the airborne animals of Jamaa.

EXPLORE JAMAA FROM ABOVE

ROYAL RIDGE

This spot is perfect for Jammers who love to fly high—especially falcons and eagles! Some birds of prey build lofty nests on cliffs or even mountain tops, called aeries. Having their homes so high up makes it tough for predators to make a meal of these birds' precious eggs. In Jamaa, soar above the treetops in Coral Canyons to the wings-only shop, Royal Ridge! Click the Sale sign and you'll be shown an exclusive selection of den items.

AWESOME ADVENTURES

As a flying animal you can go on an Adventure to The Forgotten Desert, where you search the desert floor for crystal shards the Phantoms scattered and return them for prizes.

BiRD HaBitats

Where do birds live? Sure, they spend a lot of time in the sky, but they can't nest on a cloud! In the wild, birds don't have epic dens like they do in Jamaa, so their choices are a little different than the Fantasy Castle or Enchanted Hollow. With up to 10,000 species, though, their habitats range from deserts to oceans, from forests to lakes—pretty much everywhere except the ocean floor!

PARTY IN THE SKY

Only flying animals can attend a Cloud Party. No wings, no service!

FLAMINGO

AJ Stats

INSPIRED BY:
Greater flamingo
(*Phoenicopterus roseus*)

SIGNATURE MOVE: How low can you go? As a flamingo in Jamaa, you'll play by going under a limbo stick!

INSIDER INFO: While playing on the shores of Crystal Sands, keep your eyes peeled for the flamingo so you can add it to your Journey Book page!

FLAMINGOS APPLY "MAKEUP" TO APPEAR MORE PINK.

FLAMINGOS IN AND OUT OF JAMAA ARE BEST KNOWN FOR THEIR DISTINCTIVE PINK COLORING—BUT THEY'RE NOT BORN THIS WAY! Baby flamingos are white—they develop their hot pink coloring from eating algae and shrimp. Just like in the wild, the flamingos of Jamaa rest on one leg when they're not moving.

FLAMINGOS CAN ACTUALLY RUN ON WATER! THEIR WEBBED FEET ALLOW THEM TO BUILD UP SPEED ON TOP OF THE WATER WHEN THEY TAKE OFF.

Upside-Down Eats

Flamingos have a wacky way that they eat their dinner—upside down! When these bright birds plunge their heads into their watery homes to find food, they actually twist their heads upside down, and scoop out their meal using their upper beaks like a shovel. Dig in!

TOUCAN

AJ Stats

INSPIRED BY: Toco toucan *(Ramphastos toco)*

SIGNATURE MOVE: When these flashy fliers dance, they spiral and then glide through the air with jazzy style!

INSIDER INFO: Visit the Chamber of Knowledge in the Lost Temple of Zios, read the toucan minibook, then take the quiz at the end. If you get five questions right, you get a Toucan Trophy!

WILD TOUCANS AREN'T GREAT FLIERS. THEY GENERALLY ONLY FLY SHORT DISTANCES, SOMETIMES PREFERRING TO HOP.

DO YOU LIKE TO STAND OUT? Are you playful, social, and able to learn new skills quickly? Then you should totally jam as a toucan! Toucans are recognizable by their huge, brightly colored bills, which they use to pluck fruit from branches high up in rain forest canopies in South and Central America. Toucans love rain forests, so they're right at home in the Lost Temple of Zios. As a toucan, you can also dress up and go to the Cloud Party, where you'll mingle with your other flying friends. You shouldn't brag, but as a toucan, you definitely stand out as the most fashionable—even without getting dressed!

Brilliant Beaks

Toucans primarily use their bills—which are a third of their length and serrated like a knife—to tear apart their food. They also use them to toss food to one another! Having such a big beak comes in handy. When toucans glimpse tasty morsels on a branch too small for them to land on, they stretch out to reach their meal. But despite their size, these beautiful bills are very light. The outside layer is made of keratin, the same substance that makes up your fingernails.

BiRDS OF PREY

ALSO KNOWN AS RAPTORS, BIRDS OF PREY HAVE HOOKED BEAKS, AMAZING EYESIGHT, SHARP TALONS, and strong legs and feet, which they use to swoop down and grab prey they've spotted with their excellent vision. Luckily, the raptors of Jamaa don't have to hunt, so they get to join the rest of the animals to have fun!

FALCON

DO YOU HAVE KEEN SENSES, AND ARE YOU FEARLESS IN USING THEM? You may be a falcon! These powerful birds have excellent eyesight, which they use to spot potential prey like mice, rabbits, and lizards from above. They are so bold they'll even prey on other birds while in midair! As a falcon in Jamaa you can explore everywhere but the oceans. The only time falcons don't look super fierce is when they're sleeping, which they do lying on the ground ... or even in midair! Even majestic birds of prey have to let their hair, or feathers, down sometime!

AJ Stats

INSPIRED BY: Peregrine falcon *(Falco peregrinus)*
SIGNATURE MOVE: Speaking of fierce, you haven't lived till you've seen a falcon pop and lock!
INSIDER INFO: Want to swap out the default colors on your falcon? Once you do, you can't go back!

eagle

DO YOU HAVE, WELL, EAGLE EYES?

Then you may want to fly around Jamaa as this majestic creature! Eagles' eyes are so big, they take up 50 percent of their heads, and their vision is up to five times better than that of a human. When you fly around as an eagle, you'll feel like you're getting an extra good look at all the activity happening in Jamaa. And when you see something interesting happening, click the Play button to swoop down with your talons out.

AJ Stats

INSPIRED BY: Bald eagle (*Haliaeetus leucocephalus*)
SIGNATURE MOVE: It's not exactly regal, but there's something special about an eagle snoring on top of a cloud!
INSIDER INFO: Love the game Swoopy Eagle but don't want to leave your den? Buy a Swoopy Eagle arcade machine, put it in your den, and invite your buddies over to play!

IF YOUR VISION WERE AS GOOD AS AN EAGLE'S, YOU COULD BE 100 FEET (30.5 M) IN THE AIR AND STILL SEE AN ANT ON THE GROUND.

AJ Stats

INSPIRED BY: Great horned owl (*Bubo virginianus*)
SIGNATURE MOVE: Owls dance by spinning their head around and then spinning their body around.
INSIDER INFO: They have their own video, "Out on a Limb"—watch it in the Appondale Theater.

OWL

DO YOU EVER WISH YOU HAD EYES IN THE BACK OF YOUR HEAD?

Maybe an owl is *whoo-hoo hoo* you are! Owls don't have eyes on the back of their heads, but they *can* rotate their head farther than any other animal— 270 degrees, or about three quarters of the way around! This special ability allows owls to see a lot—to the side and even behind them—without having to turn their bodies. This helps them stay out of the sight of predators. Jamaa's owls also have special head-turning skills—they can turn their heads 360 degrees (*all* the way around)— and when they play, they move their head in circles until they get so dizzy they fall over!

A GROUP OF OWLS IS CALLED A PARLIAMENT.

other COOL critters

PETS IN JAMAA ARE COMPANIONS that stick by your side wherever you go. You can choose a pet that pairs perfectly with your animals in Jamaa or you can choose a pet you like in real life! Like animals, some pets can only go in the ocean and some pets can only be with you on land. (A few pets can go on land and underwater.) And if you're a flying animal, you'll need a flying pet; otherwise, your cute companion won't be able to soar with you above Jamaa.

ADOPTING YOUR FIRST PET

To choose your pet, visit one of the pet shops in Jamaa: **Claws 'N Paws** in Appondale, **Flippers 'N Fins** in Crystal Reef (for ocean pets), or the **Diamond Shop** in Jamaa Township.

You can also find tiny icons of pets floating all over Jamaa. Click one and it will lead you to where you can adopt your new sidekick.

You can also get to pets just by going to your animal customization menu and clicking the **Pets button** at the bottom.

Next, you're taken to a menu like the menu you saw when becoming your first animal, except here, pets are displayed. From there it's just like choosing your first animal. Members get to choose any of the pets they see, though you might need Diamonds to adopt some pets.

CHOOSE YOUR PET'S LOOK

You can choose your pet's look just like you chose your own. But make sure you like the colors and features you choose for your pet, because you won't be able to change them like you can for yourself.

DECK OUT YOUR PET

After you've picked your pet's color, features, and name, swing by the **Pet Stop** to buy it accessories like purses, hats, and jewelry. Some pets even come with their own pet! Once you're finished customizing your little friend, take it to the **Pet Wash** in Crystal Sands as a final adorable touch.

Every pet has its own exclusive set of accessories.

With tons of pets to adopt, the fashion options are almost endless. Try different hats, necklaces, masks, and so much more on your cute companion.

It will cost you Gems each time you want to change the accessories on your pet.

COLOR   EYES   FEATURES

Color 1

Color 2

ONLY IN PLAY WILD

TO ADOPT A PET, VISIT THE SAPPHIRE SHOP IN JAMAA TOWNSHIP OR CLAWS 'N PAWS IN APPONDALE. YOU CAN ALSO WIN PETS IN SOME GAMES.

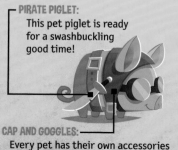

PIRATE PIGLET:
This pet piglet is ready for a swashbuckling good time!

CAP AND GOGGLES:
Every pet has their own accessories you can purchase—but there are even more options at some special parties!

59

OtHeR COOL CRitteRS

AFTER YOU'VE ADOPTED, DRESSED, and decked out your very own special sidekick, you might wonder what else you can do together. Fortunately, in Jamaa, it sometimes takes two to do some of these awesome activities.

FUn anD Games

Did you know there are special games just for pets? They aren't listed with the regular games so you'll have to find them around Jamaa. When you play those games, if you collect enough items (depending on the game), you win a special pet effect. You don't have to collect them all at once, so don't worry if you have to take a break. The next time you play, you can collect more until you get 100. Then you can collect your prize effect.

pet Prizes

If you have certain pets, you can play special games: **Disc Toss** for pet puppies, **Ducky Dash** for pet duckies, and **Sssssnake** for pet snakes. **For pet effects:** Puppies get bones, duckies get eggs, and snakes get skulls.

Pet Parties!

Jammers traveling with a pet can attend two awesome parties: the Pets Only Party and the Play-As-Your-Pet Party. While the Pets Only Party is open to all Jammers with a pet, when you attend the Play-As-Your-Pet Party, you get to see Jamaa through the eyes of your adorable companion. Both parties have special Pet Stops where you can get exclusive accessories.

Mystery Pets!

GET READY FOR AN EGGSTRAVAGANZA—PETS HATCHING FROM EGGS! Buy an egg at the Diamond Shop or at one of the nests you see around Jamaa, then customize it by changing its color and even adding a little sparkle to it. In three days it will hatch and you'll find out what your new pet is. New pets are available in the Eggstravaganza from time to time, and these fun pets can't be found anywhere else in Jamaa!

ONLY IN PLAY WILD

AT SOME SHOPS, YOU CAN ALSO BUY SPECIAL DEN ITEMS JUST FOR YOUR PET! For instance, if you buy the Puppy's Bone for your pet puppy and place it in your den, every time your pet puppy walks close, they'll play with it! Pick up some Bongo Drums for your pet bunny or a Ball of Yarn for your pet kitty—each pet has at least three pet toys they can play with when in your den.

JOURNEY BOOK

EACH LAND AND EACH OCEAN IN JAMAA IS HOME TO DIFFERENT PLANTS AND ANIMALS. One of the many fun things you can do in Jamaa is fill up your Journey Book as you spot them on your travels.

Y OU CAN ACCESS THE JOURNEY BOOK by clicking the image of a **book stamped with AJ** at the top of your screen. Click it and you'll find a book filled with outlines of animals and plants, which you try to match to the plants and animals you see around Jamaa. Each land and ocean has its own page in the Journey Book.

In your Journey Book, there are more than 100 animals and plants to find, but let's take a peek at some of the special animals from each land:

LOST TEMPLE OF ZIOS
As you make your way through lush hibiscus flowers and carnivorous pitcher plants, keep your eyes open for vine snakes! Find all the plants and animals in this jungle terrain and win an Elephant Throne.

KIMBARA OUTBACK
The lyrebird's many songs will accompany you on your adventure through this land. Be sure to avoid the venomous tiger snakes, though! Find all the plants and animals here and win a Windmill.

CORAL CANYONS
If you're journeying through these canyons, watch out for serpents such as this rattlesnake! Find all the plants and animals in this desert landscape and win a Cactus Chair.

MT. SHIVEER
Alpine-dwelling juniper trees stay green all year long, which is lucky for hawk moth larvae, which sometimes feed on their leaves. Find all the plants and animals here and win a Red Panda Plushie.

SAREPIA FOREST
The forest is home to lots of animals, from the slow-moving snail to the quick-pecking woodpecker. Find all the plants and animals in this area and win a Tree House.

APPONDALE
Savannas are home to bugs of all kinds, such as cockroaches, which have lived for at least 300 million years! Find all the plants and animals here and win an Acacia Pet Tree.

CRYSTAL SANDS
Take a break from your adventure on a white sandy shore, home to sand dollars and curious macaws that circle overhead. Find all the plants and animals here and win a Lemonade Stand.

BALLOOSH
Herons live along rivers, lakes, marshes, and swamps, where water-dwelling plants like cattails grow. Find all the plants and animals in these wetlands and win a Crescent Moon Window.

BAHARI BAY
The long "strings" you see underneath some jellyfish are tentacles. Find all the plants and animals in this watery land and win a Seahorse Fountain.

KANI COVE
Dive among the coral and you might see nautiluses, a type of mollusk that has existed for more than 400 million years. Find all the plants and animals in this aquatic area and win a Toy Boat Pond.

DEEP BLUE
Giant squid can be found at depths of up to 3,800 feet (1,158 m) beneath the waves. Find all the plants and animals here in the deep and win a Porthole Fish Tank!

CRYSTAL REEF
Clownfish, small tropical fish that make their homes on colorful coral reefs, live alongside stinging anemones. Find all the plants and animals here and win a Pufferfish Plushie.

Fantastic FASHiONS!

One of the best things about being an animal in Jamaa is dressing up. Start with the color and pattern of your fur (or feathers or scales!) and go from there. You can buy all kinds of cool accessories and clothes around Jamaa. You can make yourself look beautiful, tough, brave, sporty, or medieval! With trillions of item combinations in Jamaa, there are almost no limits to how creative you can be.

HOW to
Get Stuff

THERE ARE SO MANY WAYS TO GET FUN STUFF IN ANIMAL JAM. The currencies in Jamaa are Gems and Diamonds, and there are lots of ways to earn them, from spinning the Daily Spin to playing games. You can also get the items you want in Jamaa by trading.

ONCE YOU HAVE SOME GEMS AND DIAMONDS, you can make fashion finds at the shops all over Jamaa. You can also buy clothes or accessories at parties or trade with your buddies.

MEMBER DAILY SPIN

Click the spin button!
Log in daily to increase your bonus!

SPIN

x1 x2 x3

x 3 =

DAILY SPIN

Every day that you sign into Animal Jam, you'll see a **wheel.** When you spin it, you'll get either Gems or Diamonds. Nonmembers get the chance to earn one Diamond, 50 to 75 Gems, or a special surprise. Members get a chance to earn up to three Diamonds or a special surprise, indicated by a picture of a present. Jammers are rewarded by playing the game every day; play two days in a row and you could get two Diamonds or play three days in a row and you could get three Diamonds!

SHOP FROM THE COMFORT OF YOUR DEN!

You don't have to leave your den to dress in style. Although there isn't a shop inside your den, you can just click your picture at the bottom left of your screen, which takes you to your animal customization menu. Click the **Shop button** 🛍️ to be taken to Jam Mart Clothing, where you can buy all the fashionable duds in Jamaa. If you like something, try it on. If you still like it, you can buy it. Don't forget: You can pick the color of items before you buy them!

PARTIES

Parties are the place to snap up special items and accessories. You may see them listed in the Jamaa Journal or through your **Party List.**  You'll find a list of parties and other fun events happening at that time and later that day. There's every kind of party you can think of, from school parties to fancy dinner parties. Go to hang out with buddies, to shop, or to do both.

ONLY IN PLAY WILD

WHILE YOU USE GEMS TO PURCHASE THINGS EVERY DAY IN PLAY WILD, TO GET THE BEST ITEMS AND ANIMALS, YOU'LL NEED TO PAY WITH SAPPHIRES–THE MOBILE GAME'S SPARKLY BLUE CURRENCY.

GAMES

Many fun games are spread throughout Jamaa, and playing them is a great way to earn Gems. To find games, click the **Games icon** at the top of the screen. You can also find games all over Jamaa—just click any of the floating game icons. Some games give you the chance to earn plushies, make cotton candy, or get some other reward. Others let you earn Gems. Although some games will cost you a few Gems to play, most cost nothing at all!

Let's TALK SHOP!

IT'S TIME TO GET FASHION FORWARD! Jamaa has lots of awesome shops where you can buy clothing and accessories. Visit all the following shops to find the perfect outfit for every occasion.

DIAMOND SHOP

Located right in the center of Jamaa Township is the Diamond Shop. This amazing shop is filled with all the latest and greatest animals, pets, dens, accessories, and den items. Stop on by to see all the incredible things for sale!

BAHARI BARGAINS

Located in the center of Bahari Bay, built on a rocky outcrop, this is the place to find all the latest in underwater items and accessories. And for some extra sparkle, be sure to visit the Bahari Bargains Diamond Shop.

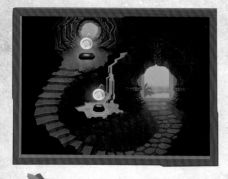

EPIC WONDERS

Epic Wonders is a shop that's so cool, it's found behind a waterfall in Coral Canyons. This is the place to go when Gems are burning a hole in your pocket! Want a Tuxedo for 7,500 Gems? What about a Golden Unicorn Horn for 3,500 Gems?

HOSPITAL SHOP

In the heart of Kimbara Outback is Gabby's Animal Hospital. Inside the hospital, click Sale sign to find cool items to help you dress up like a doctor (maybe try the Stethoscope) or a patient (try something like a Cone Collar, Bandage, or Cast).

JAM MART CLOTHING

Located in Jamaa Township, just above the Sol Arcade, this is the shop where most of Jamaa's land clothing and accessories are sold. **HOT TIP:** This is also where Rare Item Monday clothing items are often sold.

Rare Item

OUTBACK IMPORTS

Carved into a cliffside in Kimbara Outback, this shop offers Jammers another place to purchase cool stuff for their dens. Think you'd like a Stone Carved Chair, Table, or Couch? Swing by the Outback!

MUSEUM SHOP

Whenever you feel a need to update your hat, you only need to pop by this shop housed in the Conservation Museum in the center of Appondale. Inside you'll find some of the best animal-themed hats that Gems can buy!

SHIVEER SHOPPE

Found on the chilly slopes of Mt. Shiveer, this shop is cozily tucked into the Hot Cocoa Hut. Click the Sale sign inside and choose from a variety of cold-weather items and accessories. And don't forget to treat yourself to a hot cocoa before facing the elements!

PET STOP

You weren't going to forget about your pet, were you? After you've found your new faithful companion at Claws 'N Paws in Appondale or at the Flippers 'N Fins in Crystal Reef, stop by to accessorize them with clothes and accessories—or to get them a special treat!

ANCIENT ARMORY

If you want to look the way some of the ancient animals of Jamaa would have, pick up the Ancient Armor from this Balloosh shop located inside the Temple of the Ancients.

ONLY IN PLAY WILD

THE SAPPHIRE SHOP IS THE PLACE TO FIND ALL THE LATEST LOOKS AND ACCESSORIES IN PLAY WILD. Located in Jamaa Township, this shop is bursting with awesome ways to show off your style! Can't find what you're looking for? You can also shop at Jam Mart Clothing, the Shiveer Shoppe, Epic Wonders, and Claws 'N Paws for your pets. And don't forget to keep your eyes open for the traveling salesman, a raccoon with a red fez and a wonderful pop-up shop! He shows up in different places at different times in Jamaa, selling cool stuff you can't find anywhere else.

TRADING

TRADING IS A SUPERFUN WAY TO UPDATE YOUR LOOK. There are many ways to do it. You may have noticed as you walk around Jamaa the bubbles above animals saying things like, "Trade with me plz." This means just what it says—that Jammers want to trade! You may also notice the Trade icon ⟳ floating next to your buddies. This means they are in the middle of a trade!

BEFORE YOU CAN TRADE, YOU HAVE TO HAVE SOMETHING TO TRADE FOR. Go to your **animal customization menu** and click the **Trade tab** at the top. Then click the **plus button** ⊕. It will take you to your items so you can look through and decide what you are ready to let go of. Once you decide, just click it and it will be added to your **Trade List!**

TRADE LIST:
You can put accessories and den items on your trade list.

ADD tO TRADE LiST

Wanna Trade?

Q Search...   **SORT**

SORT:
Use the Sort and Search options to quickly find that special item that you're looking for.

When someone asks if anyone wants to trade, click their name tag to bring up their **Player Card**. Click the **Trade tab** and their **Trade List** will pop up. You can scroll through it and see if there's anything you'd like to trade for. If there is, click it, then click the **plus button**  and add what you would like to trade for.

REMEMBER, JAMMERS:

Trading is permanent, so only trade items you are sure you want to get rid of. Sometimes people may say things like "trust trade" or "let me try it on," or they may want you to trade them through Jam-A-Grams. If you see one of these Jammers, it's not a good idea to trade with them. The Trading System exists to keep all trades fair, and smart Jammers always use it!

TRADE WITH ANY PLAYER:

The Trading System is a safe and fair way to trade with other Jammers, even if they're not your Buddies. This is where you'll see who you're trading with.

YOUR ITEM:

This is where you'll see the item you're trading.

TRADE REQUESTED

New Jammer wants to trade their **6 items**

for your

Precious Snowflake

6 items

Do you want to trade?

TRADE CANCEL

WHAT YOU'LL GET:

Jammers can offer up to 20 items to trade.

ACCEPT OR CANCEL:

Ready to accept or walk away? Click these buttons to end the trading session.

73

RecyclinG

WHEN YOU'RE OFFLINE, ONE WAY TO LET GO OF CLOTHES AND ACCESSORIES YOU DON'T WEAR ANYMORE IS TO RECYCLE THEM. You can donate your clothes to a charitable organization or bring them to a second-hand store that can give you money for them, and in Jamaa, you can do the same thing.

I**F YOU WANT TO RECYCLE AN ITEM**, go to your animal customization menu and click the **Recycle icon** at the bottom.

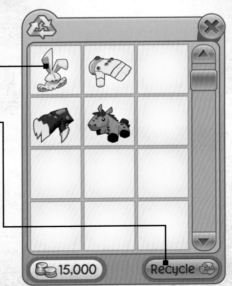

ALL OF YOUR ITEMS WILL POP UP. Click one to see how many Gems you'll get if you recycle it.

IF YOU DECIDE TO RECYCLE AN ITEM, click it and you'll get a prompt asking you if you're sure you want to. If you are, click OK and you'll receive Gems!

15,000   Recycle

RECYCLING JUST ONE SODA CAN SAVES ENOUGH ENERGY TO RUN A TV FOR THREE HOURS!

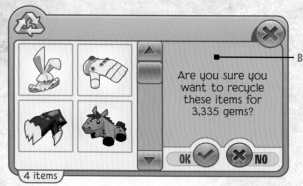

Are you sure you want to recycle these items for 3,335 gems?

OK ✓   ✗ NO

4 items

BE CAREFUL, THOUGH:
Even if you're recycling a Diamond item, you'll get Gems in return. And remember: Once you recycle an item, it's gone for good, so be sure you only recycle items you don't want anymore.

Recycled Fashion

One of the reasons it's important to recycle or trade your clothes is because it's good for the environment: The more new clothes being made, the more the Earth's limited resources are used. To show support for animals and to encourage humans to live more sustainably, wildlife veterinarian and eco-friendly fashionista, Dr. Gabby Wild decided to wear only one garment for an entire month! Gabby hopes to merge fashion and science to help spread the word about conservation and encourage sustainable practices that will help our animal friends.

There are many ways to be a fashion activist. Did you know some people even recycle non-clothes into clothes? People have made clothes from plastic bottles, bamboo, and even coffee grounds!

INSIDER INFO

SOMETIMES IT'S A GOOD IDEA TO HANG ON TO ITEMS INSTEAD OF RECYCLING THEM. You never know when an old item will suddenly come back in style, and there may be an item that comes out in the future that is the perfect match for one of your older accessories.

Best Dressed

THIS POPULAR GAME IS THE ONLY ONE IN JAMAA THAT CAN BE PLAYED BOTH ON LAND AND IN THE OCEAN! To play Best Dressed, click the Game icon at the top of the screen. You can also play this game in Coral Canyons, the Sol Arcade, and Bahari Bay.

ONCE YOU ENTER THE GAME, YOU'LL NEED TO WAIT FOR A NEW ROUND. Use this time to practice for the upcoming game. When the game starts, you'll find yourself in a darkened stage area. An envelope will appear with directions for your costume. It can be anything from "Most Futuristic" to "Most Like a Sea Monster."

Dress Your Best

Practice dressing your best while you wait for the next round!

OKay

NEW THEME!

Dress up the NEATEST

General Jazzyroo

0:34

CLOTHES

Rare

Rare

Rare

Color 1

Color 2

SORT BY..

Dress up the SCARIEST

FASHION ITEMS SORT BY CATEGORY:
Using the **sort button** at the bottom of the screen will help you use your time efficiently. You can sort by head, neck, back, legs, oldest, and newest.

SCROLL UP AND DOWN FOR MORE

TIMER: You have only a short time to come up with the perfect costume for the theme, so think fast!

PICK COLORS AND PATTERNS from the customization menu.

CLICK HERE WHEN DONE!

Best Dressed

Vote! Vote! Vote! Vote! Vote! Vote! Vote! Vote! Vote!

Waiting for others... FREAKIEST

O NCE THE TIME IS UP, YOU'LL RETURN TO THE STAGE TO VOTE AND BE VOTED ON! You'll get to see everyone's costume choices and decide which you think is best. **(Pro tip: You can't vote for yourself.)**

Then a big scroll will appear and will show how everyone ranked and how many Gems they got!

VOTING TIMER: Don't forget to vote; otherwise, you won't win any Gems! When the winners are announced, you'll see a 1st, 2nd, and 3rd place banner under the winners—there may be multiple winners at each level.

FIRST PLACE ALWAYS GETS
200 Gems, and everyone else gets between 25 and 150 Gems depending on how many Jammers are playing.

ROUND RESULTS

Rank	Name	Votes	Gems
1.	Magical Grandpaw	3	200
2.	Commander Peachyproud	2	150
2.	Count Frillymush	2	150
3.	Baron Peachycloud	1	100
3.	Captain Fancykoala	1	100
3.	Old Canyonrose	1	100
4.	Fabulous Sunnybrave	0	25
4.	Laughing Stinkypanda	0	25
4.	Sparkle Loudpirate	0	25
4.	Mighty Smellylily	0	25

LAND ACHIEVEMENTS

50

SEAMSTRESS!
Play Best Dressed
5 times

STYLIST!
Play Best Dressed
10 times

DESIGNER!
Play Best Dressed
25 times

MODEL!
Play Best Dressed
50 times

HIGH FASHION!
Win 20 rounds of
Best Dressed

TRES CHIC!
Win 3 rounds in a row
in one game of Best
Dressed

OCEAN ACHIEVEMENTS

250

SHARP!
Play Best Dressed
(Oceans) 5 times

CLASSY!
Play Best Dressed
(Oceans) 10 times

POSH!
Play Best Dressed
(Oceans) 25 times

ELEGANT!
Play Best Dressed
(Oceans) 50 times

DASHING!
Win 20 rounds of Best
Dressed (Oceans)

IN VOGUE!
Win 3 rounds in a row
in one game of Best
Dressed (Oceans)

CELEBRATE IN STYLE

THERE'S NO SHORTAGE OF OCCASIONS TO CELEBRATE IN JAMAA! Whether it's a festival, celebration, or themed party, there's always something to swap your style for.

YOU CAN DRESS FOR WHATEVER OCCASION YOU WANT TO CELEBRATE; there are lots of cool looks that you can sport for different celebrations. When Lucky Day rolls around, you could buy some Clover Earmuffs or a Clover Top Hat—you can even wear a Clover Antenna Headband. For the Feast of Thanks, maybe get yourself a Feather Mask or a Turkey Hat!

NIGHT OF THE PHANTOMS

During the month of October, be prepared for Jamaa to get a little dark and spooky—but always fun! Check out this cool outfit inspiration for this special fall holiday.

SPOOKY COLORS: Accessorizing can go beyond just adding a hat! Try changing up your colors for the full effect.

PET PARTICIPATION: Boost your festive fashion by accessorizing your pet, too!

CELEBRATIONS

FRIENDSHIP FESTIVAL
(February)

CHINESE NEW YEAR
(February)

SAFER INTERNET DAY
(February)

CARNIVAL
(February)

INTERNATIONAL POLAR BEAR DAY
(February)

LUCKY DAY
(March)

PI DAY
(March)

APRIL FOOLS' DAY
(April)

EARTH DAY
(April)

WORLD OCEANS DAY
(June)

MAKE MUSIC DAY
(June)

FREEDOM DAY
(July)

NATIONAL HONEYBEE DAY
(August)

WORLD RHINO DAY
(September)

WORLD ANIMAL DAY
(October)

NIGHT OF THE PHANTOMS
(October)

FEAST OF THANKS
(November)

JAMAALIDAYS
(series of celebrations during the winter)

CHINESE NEW YEAR

The Chinese New Year, also called the Spring Festival, is one of the most celebrated holidays in the world. Join the celebration with these fun Emperor and Empress outfits, available only in Play Wild!

MIXING OLD AND NEW: These ornate outfits both capture the traditional spirit of Asia's rich cultural heritage, but the pop of bright color on the Empress outfit adds a bit of modern flair!

AMAZING LOOKS

JAMAA HAS SOME FABULOUS FASHIONISTAS, AND WILDLIFE VETERINARIAN DR. GABBY WILD LOVES TO BE INSPIRED BY THEIR FANTASTIC LOOKS! Whenever she can, she finds Jammers who take their style to the next level.

TOTALLY TURQUOISE

COLORS, EYES & PATTERN:
Jammers with an eye for style will often change their colors, eyes, and pattern to match the items they're wearing.

FEATHERED MASK:
Headed to a masquerade? You'll be in fine feather with this dazzling headpiece!

DR. GABBY'S TREND TIPS:
Fashion is a great way to get people's attention—whether to raise awareness about animals or just for fun—and this beautiful blue look sure is eye-catching!

TURQUOISE BRACELET:
This stunning bracelet features a turquoise gemstone. Turquoise has been used since ancient times—the Maya ruled that no one was allowed to wear it because it was used as an offering to the gods. But in Jamaa, you can deck yourself out in as much as you want!

WINGED WARRIOR

MECH ANGEL HELMET:
You won't be overlooked in this golden helmet! It features a leaf-adorned crest, and comes in eight different colors. Warriors throughout history are no strangers to helmet decor. Greek soldiers used crests to make themselves look taller and fiercer in battle.

CUPID WINGS:
Wings aren't just for flying! These fantastic feathery features sit high on your back and come in a variety of colors you can switch up based on your mood.

LEG ARMOR:
Add just a touch of wild to your look with this gorgeous leaf leg armor.

PURR-FECT PATTERN:
Most Jammers never want to blend in with the crowd. But just in case of an emergency, these bold spiral patterns will camouflage you and keep you out of sight!

DR. GABBY'S TREND TIPS: Every animal knows how to stay on their guard! Whether it's big, beautiful colors and crests to stand out or funky spots and stripes that help them hide, these trendsetters know how to use fashion to protect themselves and others.

83

SOPHISTICATED SWIMMER

JELLYFISH HAT:

Is that a jelly on your head? Absolutely! This quirky hat comes with six tentacles that are just the right length. Some wild jellies have tentacles that could stretch more than the length of a basketball court!

SEAWEED BOA:

You'll be dazzling and divine in this fantastic members-only neck piece! This beautiful boa comes in eight different colors. If you're lucky and are on the lookout, you might also be able snag a Rare Seaweed Boa.

PET ACCESSORIES:

These exclusive pet hippo headband and necklace options will elevate your pet's wildest look.

DR. GABBY'S TREND TIPS: Animals are the ultimate fashion trendsetters! For millions of years, animals have made their surroundings into fabulous fashion accessories. Bright and colorful coral fish might try to stand out or camo crabs might grab shells off the ocean floor to decorate their homes.

INSIDER INFO

EVERY PET IN JAMAA HAS ITS OWN SPECIAL FASHION OPTIONS! Pop over to the Pet Stop with your sidekick and start styling. With tons of pets to adopt in Jamaa, the options are almost endless.

HORNED HERO

SHARK HAT:
Chomp on this! This ferocious Shark Hat comes complete with everything you need to look your fiercest—sharp teeth and even a fin! Plus, this hat's dark eyes always stay open, just like wild sharks (they can't blink!).

JAGGED SWIRL PATTERN:
Check out this awesome addition to the super cool rhino horn! Patterns and colors give this fierce piece an extra edge that will definitely get you noticed.

STEGOSAURUS TAIL:
Give your look a prehistoric vibe with the Stegosaurus Tail! Three spikes along the top will make your look sharper than ever!

DR. GABBY'S TREND TIPS: Trendsetters know how to go big or go home! But you don't always have to add a ton of stuff to your look to make it great. Try adding subtle details—like beads, a hint of color, or a bit of faux fur—to take your look to a whole other level!

85

PINK POWER

HAUTE HAT:
Try a Top Hat on for size! This classy hat is a hit with Jammers—it's one of the most popular items. In fact, U.S. president Abraham Lincoln liked his top hat so much he kept important papers inside it. In Jamaa, the hat comes in different colors, but depending on the season, there may be different, special versions, like this Rare Friendship Hat!

THERE ARE TONS OF PINK THINGS IN NATURE, SUCH AS IGUANAS, BLUEBERRIES, SAPPHIRES, LAKES, AND MORE! TALK ABOUT PINK POWER!

HEART LOCKET:
Lock in the love with this dazzling Heart Locket! This beauty comes in eight different colors, so you can mix and match, depending on your mood.

WILD WINGS:
Ready to hit the skies? Even if you're a land animal you can be in style with these Rare Friendship Wings.

HEART BOOTS:
You can never have too many shoes in Jamaa— so show your feet lots of love! These gorgeous Heart Boots come in eight different colors you can switch up anytime you want a new look.

 DR. GABBY'S TREND TIPS: Animals have the perfect balance of fashion and friendship! Consider making new friends at Jamaa's Friendship Festival, held during the month of February. You never know what new sensational styles you might learn from your new pals!

86

WONDERFUL WIZARD

RARE NERD GLASSES:
Think glasses for animals is strange? Think again! Some chickens wear safety glasses! But for a more stylish look, stick with these nerd-tastic glasses—you'll be the smartest-looking Jammer in Jamaa. Pair these rare frames with any of your awesome looks and stand out from the crowd.

GRADUATION GOWN:
Try your hand at a disappearing act in this mysterious members-only gown. It comes in several different colors to mix and match if you're feeling daring.

TIE: Look super spiffy and in charge with the tiest tie of all ties. Yes, it has patches, but that's because it stays busy "tieing" everyone's look together!

INSIDER INFO

SOME ANIMALS GET A KICK OUT OF CHANGING THEIR LOOK! Try swapping patterns, changing colors, and adding new accessories to make your look match your awesome personality.

DR. GABBY'S TREND TIPS:
Fashionistas can be mysterious, just like some animals! Blend into corners like a snake with darker colors and patterns or get serene like an owl with vibrant eyes and big, soft feathers.

SAVE THE ANIMALS

LIKE ALL JAMMERS, YOU'RE A FRIEND TO ANIMALS. And you probably love them even more after having learned so much about their lives in Jamaa and in the wild. There are lots of ways you can work to help animals in your own neighborhood and across the globe. Here are some ideas to get you started:

1

HOST YOUR OWN BEST DRESSED PARTY where you and your friends dress up like your favorite animals. Or take an idea from Animal Jam and have a big box of costumes and accessories to choose from and then give each friend five minutes to put together an outfit, like Dress the Weirdest Animal, the Coolest Animal, or the Most Like a Bug or a Bird! Ask your friends to each bring a can of pet food to donate to your local shelter.

HOST A CLEANUP DAY and invite your family and friends to join you.

HAVE A BAKE SALE AND DONATE THE PROFITS to an animal or environmental conservation group.

WRITE A REPORT ABOUT CONSERVATION and the importance of saving animals' habitats, and share it with your class at school.

FINAL WORDS FROM

ANIMAL JAM

WE'RE SO GLAD THAT YOU'VE CHOSEN TO ENTER THE WORLD OF ANIMAL JAM! It's so cool to see kids who love animals as much as you do. We know you're going to have an amazing time going on Adventures, making buddies, learning about animals, and exploring the fantastic world of Jamaa!

Now that you know all about the animals you can become in Jamaa, it's time to jump in feetfirst. There's a whole world of animal adventures awaiting you. Get out there and play wild!

—Animal Jam

INDEX

INDEX

CREDITS

Since 1888, the National Geographic Society has funded more than 12,000 research, exploration, and preservation projects around the world. The Society receives funds from National Geographic Partners, LLC, funded in part by your purchase. A portion of the proceeds from this book supports this vital work. To learn more, visit natgeo.com/info.

For more information, visit nationalgeographic.com, call 1-800-647-5463; or write to the following address:

National Geographic Partners
1145 17th Street N.W.
Washington, D.C. 20036-4688 U.S.A.

Visit us online at:
nationalgeographic.com/books

For librarians and teachers:
ngchildrensbooks.org

More for kids from National Geographic:
natgeokids.com

For information about special discounts for bulk purchases, please contact National Geographic Books Special Sales: specialsales@natgeo.com

For rights or permissions inquiries, please contact National Geographic Books Subsidiary Rights: bookrights@natgeo.com

Designed by Stephanie White

The publisher would like to thank the following people for making this book possible: Kate Hale, executive editor; Callie Broaddus, senior designer; Sarah J. Mock, senior photo editor; Girl Friday Productions, editorial direction; Jen Agresta, contributing writer; Alix Inchausti, production editor; Paige Towler, associate editor; Michelle Tyler, editorial assistant; and Anne LeongSon and Gus Tello, production assistants. Special thanks to the entire staff of creative and production teams at WildWorks, Inc.

Hardcover ISBN: 978-1-4263-3144-2
Reinforced library binding ISBN: 978-1-4263-3145-9

Printed in China
18/RRDH/1